The Science of Artificial Intelligence – Part 1 – Mastering the Quantitative Learning Surface

By Michael Sinyangwe

In 2019

NOTA BENE: If any organisation/individual wants to use any of the natural language text, code, tables, or images, in this Obsidian Oblation book (or any similar such things) in any of their internal/external books/products/services/experiences, then they must agree to, and are indeed bound by the Almighty God under Wrath of punishment, to do the following 3 things: 1. Make reference to me (actual name, Literary name (Caramel Cocoa Brownie), and Obsidian Oblation... logo optional) as the originator of core natural language text, code, tables, or images in the internal/external book/product/service/experience, within the internal/external book/product/service/experience itself in a prominent position; 2. Make ongoing total monthly donations of 1% of all income{costs plus contingent}/revenue (whichever is greatest) generated by all of your internal/external books/products/services/Experiences which use any of the natural language text, code, tables, or images in this Obsidian Oblation book (or any similar such things), to any Catholic Charities of your choice who are part of the Catholic Church's Obsidian Caritas Social Action Network of official Catholic Charities; 3. Include this nota bene in a prominent position in all documentation/code scripts that use any of the natural language text, code, tables, or images in this Obsidian Oblation book (or any similar such things)... Moreover, if you use any ideas, concepts, or algorithmic designs within this Obsidian Oblation book, that are conveyed to you in non-computer code language (e.g. natural human language or images etc.), in any of your internal/external books/products/services/experiences, then I strongly exhort you to donate that 1% of total ongoing income{costs plus contingent}/revenue generated, to any Catholic Charities of your choice who are part of the Catholic Church's Obsidian Caritas Social Action Network of official Catholic Charities. This licence can be withdrawn from any individual and/or organisation, and thereby cancelled, on a case-by-case basis,

Contents

The Nomenclature

- **AI System** – This term defines all the human, physical, and technological resources and their processes of interaction, which are involved throughout the whole AI lifecycle, from design, to develop, to operate, and cycling back again.
- **Convolutional Neural Network** – This term is the name of the quantitative machine learning model which is outlined in this book.
- **Game** – This term defines a major artificial intelligence challenge that repeatedly needs to be solved throughout the AI system. There are many solutions for each game, each with its own set of advantages and disadvantages.
- **Infrastructure** – This term defines the configuration of the software and hardware used to run a solution, module, or package.
- **Solution** – This term defines the totality of the configuration and code of modules contained in the core of an AI system.
- **Module** – This term defines a group of packages that perform major functions within the solution.
- **Package** – This term defines the algorithms, techniques, and methods, which as a group, have an important function within a module.
- **Algorithm** – This term describes a chain of techniques which produce a result set.
- **Technique** – This term defines a set of methodical data processing steps.
- **Method** – This term defines, in coding phraseology, the data input, the operation, and the data output of one transformation step in a given technique.

The Theory of Correlation, Cause, and Effect

What is Correlation?

Correlation is not the same as causation. Correlation simply describes how one variable moves, on average, compared to another variable. This does not on its own mean that a variable has caused another variable to change. Cause-effect analysis requires a more nuanced approach. There are two possible outcomes of a cause-effect analysis. Either the analysed cause variable is causing the effect variable to change purely due to a random coincidence, or the effect variable has changed due to randomicity in the change of the cause variable. If it is the former outcome, then there is no cause-effect relationship that can be discovered, and therefore the application of any correlation would lead to errors in the package's outputs. If it is the later outcome, then there is a cause-effect relationship that can be discovered, and therefore the application of any correlation would lead to an effective projection of the effect variable, to a certain degree of accuracy, given other package data and mechanics.

Cause-Effect Modelling

Put simply, if a cause variable branches significantly from the mean gradient, it is a candidate for a randomly caused differential, and could therefore be removed from the inputs of a specific projected data point. Otherwise if a cause variable converges significantly with the mean gradient, it is a candidate for a randomicitly caused differential, and could therefore be included in the inputs of a specific projected data point. The question is, how do you decide the degree of branching or converging that is optimal for a given projection? You need to design thresholds for maximum and minimum branching/converging for input selection, which are based on the human user's risk appetite, so that they can adjust the amount of uncertainty in the projection, based on the movement of these thresholds. Alternatively, the change in these thresholds could be machine learnt.

Is It Possible to Spot and Deal with Random Coincidence?

If you include a new observation, and the correlation between the input and output variables becomes significantly 'disloyal', while all other related correlations remain significantly and comparatively 'loyal', then this is a candidate for a random correlation coincidence. In such cases, the observation in question should be removed from the inputs of the correlation for a given set of variables, but it doesn't need to be completely removed from the inputs of all correlations.

Is There a Benefit In Analysis of Correlations of Correlations?

One example where this may be useful, is when you want to allow your solution to react to changing cause-effect relationships between multiple layers in various hierarchies of input and output variables. For example, in Q1, a stock increased 5% mainly because of an increase in available credit, but in Q2 that same relationship has changed because of another underlying relationship between interest rates and their underlying relationship with inflation and GDP. As you can see, as a solution matures, it will likely end up with many layers of related projections, within multiple hierarchies. The crucial thing to do when taking a correlation of a correlation however, is to weight the correlations, so that there is no under or over representation of lower correlations as they flow up the hierarchy. If you discover that the value of a correlation of a correlation has changed significantly, then you have to assume that the real-world conditions have changed, and therefore it would be prudent to give more emphasis to dimensionality rather than correlation, because the mean will no longer be precise enough. We need a more precise average, and this is achieved through playing the dimensionality game which I will explain later in this document.

The Games We Play Are AI Okay

When training an AI system, there are many, many, games that could be 'played'.

The Translation Game

Each AI system contains a whole panoply of coordinating nodes which interact in all sorts of fantastic ways in order to project into the future. The current form factor of physical processors, and indeed quantum processors leads to an unnecessary 'overheating' because of wastage. Here, the 'resistance' can be overcome through quantum hardware architecture functionality. The best hardware should be smart i.e. include its own AI system, as frequently modifiable as possible, and low energy consuming. It must be able to mimic the software architecture as it morphs, rather than forcing the software architecture to fit inside the hardware architecture's unchanging constraints. Essentially, you want to be able to replicate your software architecture directly into the hardware at any given point in time, with absolute fidelity.

The Priming Game

To achieve optimal performance i.e. the AI system is effective, efficient, accurate, and precise, it should be constantly aware of context, and therefore continually update its selection of dimensional layer labels with which it filters any input observations. These labels should be appropriate for the intended use of the AI system in that instance. For example, if an automated car is starting from a city centre multi-storey car park as opposed to a suburban curb-side, then the observation label filters for start, city-centre, and multi-storey carpark, should be automatically detected through GPS and other sensors. The AI system should then update its observation priming filters, calculate any outputs, and then act on those outputs. This is an ongoing cycle, and depending on the situation, it may need to happen with hyper-rapidity, or maybe in some cases much less often. As a result of this usual need for hyper-rapidity, the developer of an AI system should design it in such a way that there are sets of cached correlations (from the correlation game which I will describe later in this document), and sets of cached manipulations (from the dimensionality game which I will also describe later in this document).

The Combinations Game

For each extra observation, the possible combinations of outputs increases 'exponentially'. This game can be 'won' through the use of highly modifiable parallel scaling architecture, in software that is able to optimise linear multivariate gradients, as well as non-linear multivariate gradients, discrete multivariate 'gradients', and radial non-linear multivariate gradients.

The Resonance Game

Every solution will have to deal with the reality of inherent model weakness. This is because the techniques used to 'win' a game pass on their weaknesses to the whole solution. Thankfully, there are two sub-games within the super game, with opposing weaknesses, and therefore by 'winning' both games, you can strengthen you solution by making it more resonant, and thereby offset the inherent weaknesses in using either one individually. These sub-games are:

1. The Statistical Impartiality Game – Overcoming statistical model impartiality can be achieved by implementing a sum-of methodology. This compensates

for expectation under-confidence. The appropriate
game to overcome this impartiality is the correlation
learning game.

2. The Calculation Bias Game – Overcoming calculation
   model bias can be achieved by implementing a subtract-
   of methodology. This compensates for expectation
   over-confidence. The appropriate game to overcome
   this bias is the dimensionality learning game.

Essentially, in sum-of methodology, the more you repeat a
forecast (echo a forecast average), the more accurate your
projection will be. In relation to this, in subtract-of
methodology, the more you loosen a calculation (silence a
prediction average), the more precise your projection will be.

The Correlation Learning Game

Every solution will have to deal with the reality of branching vs.
converging observations. The best configuration of your
solution for this game, would need to allow the classification of
observations so that you can more suitably determine which
should feed into the projection of a particular future data point.
There are actually two sub-games within this super game. They
are:

1. The Noise Game – Noise exacerbation can occur from
   picking too many asymmetrically causatory input
   variables. Here, the resistance can be overcome
   through cause correlation modelling of the data
   sources.
2. The Blurring Game – Blurring exacerbation can occur
   from picking too many asymmetrically effectual output
   variables. Here, the resistance can be overcome
   through effect correlation modelling of the data
   outputs.

The Discrete Correlation Learning Game

This game is useful whenever you have an input or output whose value set is 'limited' and discrete. It allows you to treat things such as picklists of categories or status icons, similarly to how you would treat a normal rational number in the linear/non-linear correlation learning games. The steps are as follows:

1. Appropriately order the picklist. The ordering should make logical sense wherever possible, but it doesn't always have to, because you may just want to classify future observations that aren't ordinal in any reasonable way. If using a non-ordinal picklist, it is wise to incorporate as many independent variables as is appropriate, so that the chances of miss-classification are minimised. I hypothesise, that for every additional independent variable filter in a discrete dependent multivariate regression for a particular independent variable, the miss-classification rate may approximately half. When trying to 'order' an assumed non-ordinal picklist, it is wise to do an exploratory study to see if the dependent non-ordinal picklist values do or do not actually exhibit a previously unrealised sense of ordinality for a given independent variable; if no ordinality is found, then the best policy is to omit analysis of that particular dependent picklist variable/independent variable combination.

2. Assign a symmetrically increasing or decreasing number to each successive pick value in the ordered picklist, depending on which direction you want the conversion picklist to be analysed on a given axis. For example, the numbers 1 to 5 for a five category picklist.

3. Use this new correlation-ready value to feed into the linear/non-linear correlation learning game.
4. When viewing the output, use the conversion mapping to reverse map the correlation-ready value back to its original picklist value.

When dealing with an ordinal classification, if an observation is equally spaced between two classes, you should create a temporary, extra hybrid class which is assigned only to these exception case observations. This should then temporarily be dealt with as a separate class in its own right, but as a data scientist, it would be prudent to recommend a reassessment of the appropriate classes in the picklist for that variable. If you have truly multimodal data (the ideal data to use with the discrete correlation learning game), creating hybrid classes usually shouldn't be necessary.

The Non-Linear Correlation Learning and Granularity Games

This game allows you to better fit the gradient to data which is non-linear, and therefore is poorly analysed by a linear gradient calculation. The idea is that you are going to need to break up your observations into groups, and then find the non-linear gradient based on the average values of these groups. The steps are as follows:

1. Before you do anything in a non-linear correlation regression cycle, you need to find the average output value for each overall observed input value. These averages then feed into the next step as the analysed observations, but they must first be weighted by the number of observations that were collapsed into the average figure. Kudos for anyone who can tell the

lecturer why this is a necessary step, and why this is also a good step.

2. Order these (average) observations from lowest to highest input value.

3. Add a granularity variable with a minimum value of 3, which allows you to control the observation group size.

4. Assign group numbers to each observation in a group, based on the total number of observations in a group being derived from the granularity variable, so that you end up with uniform numbers within a group, and ascending numbers across groups.

5. For the penultimate group, it is necessary to include logic to check for any remaining observations which are in a group of two or less. If there are any, these need to be added to now make the last group, which was previously the penultimate group.

6. Calculate the weighted average input and output values for each group.

7. Draw the non-linear gradient through the group averages (this gradient should have noticeable corners with small datasets or extremely large group sizes).

For the end user, the smaller the configured group size, the more granular and therefore effective the technique will be at allowing you to forecast an output variable. The drawback is that as the group size gets smaller, there are more groups to calculate the gradient from, and so the technique loses efficiency. This means the projection has to become less frequent in time. Also, if it is too granular, then your system will experience over-fitting problems. There is a balance that must be struck depending on the overall granularity posture of the user's other thresholds. Obviously, if the user requires more efficiency, then they should increase the configured group size, but this will reduce forecast precision, at the same time as increasing accuracy.

In order to use this non-linear gradient, you need to make use of trigonometry theory. The steps are as follows:

8. You need to start off by finding the preceding and following-group weighted average input and output values.

9. Then take the preceding-group weighted average input value away from the following-group weighted average input value. This will give you the input length of the triangle.

10. Then, take the preceding-group weighted average output value away from the following-group weighted average output value. This will give you the output length of the triangle.

11. Pythagoras theorem ($a^2 + b^2 = c^2$), where c is the length of the gradient line hypotenuse, assures us that the sides of a triangle are proportional. Therefore we know that any reduction in one length, will proportionately reduce the lengths of the other sides of the triangle.

12. Putting this into practice, we can therefore work out the forecast output value for any given input value within an inter-group input value range.

13. To do this, for each variable, take the new input value away from its respective following-group weighted average input value.

14. Divide this differential by its respective inter-group weighted average input value length.

15. This gives us a percentage change for the new input value, with respect to its inter-group weighted average input value length.

16. Now we can multiply this percentage change value, by its respective inter-group weighted average output value length, in order to get the proportional output value change.

17. We then take this overall output value change away from the following-group weighted average output value, to find the forecast output value which intersects the new input value along the non-linear gradient 'curve'.

These 17 steps comprise a regression cycle. It is necessary however, to keep repeating this regression cycle, until all the unwanted associated observations are eliminated from the regression calculation. The exclusion should happen based on an output axis threshold which is applied across all the observed values on the input axis. A minimum of two regression cycles should be carried out before the regression curve is fit for purpose. We know it is fit for purpose, because after excluding observations in between cycles, if the curve no longer changes, it can be considered to optimally fit the data, and the 'question' you are asking of the data (the observation exclusion thresholds, and the degree of granularity variable for group size). These questions should be in harmony with the rest of the AI system in terms of accuracy (exclusion threshold), precision (group size variable), and efficiency (hardware and software, configuration and resources assigned to this particular game set), in order to meet requirements.

Once you have your final 'curve', if you need to forecast the output value for an input value that lies outside the 'curve' range, then you simply extrapolate, by using the average of the population gradient and the nearest following-pair of group averages, if your input value is before the 'curve' boundary; and by using the average of the population gradient and the nearest preceding-pair of group averages, if your input value is beyond the 'curve' boundary. The calculation is similar yet somewhat different. Kudos for anyone who can work it out.

The Linear Correlation Learning Game

Instead of using the widely standardised least mean squares approach to calculate the regression curve for linear data. I suggest just using the non-linear technique that I have outlined above. The reason is, that when you have large amounts of observations, I believe my technique can be more efficiently optimised than any adapted least mean squares technique. The configuration of the granularity threshold would have to be set so that only two groups get formed during each regression cycle.

The Radial Non-Linear Correlation Learning Game

In a few cases, you may encounter observations which are spread in a radial pattern (like a circle). To deal with this situation, you first need to split the observations in half along the linear regression curve, based on at least two dimensional label values. You then assign an additional classification value of -1 to the data set below the regression curve on the output axis, and a value of 1 to the data set above the regression curve on the output axis. In this way you are adding another variable to the regression analysis. You perform the standard non-linear correlation learning game, as outlined above, for each of these two half-datasets separately. Essentially you have split the single correlation for the one variable pair, into two correlations. After this, you simply split all incoming observations along this axis and, assign them either a -1 or 1 appropriately, which would then feed them into the most suitable sub regression analysis. After the split non-linear regression analysis, for display purposes, it is advised that you then combine the two analyses together i.e. two regression curves, along with their respective input observations. For any observation which lies exactly on the regression curve, this should be given a value of 0, and a weighting of 0.5, and so it would have a partial effect on both sub regression analyses, without being 'double counted'.

The Regular Dimensionality Learning and Granularity Games

Every solution will have to deal with dimensionality. To 'win' this game, you essentially have to mine 'transactional' data to find patterns which represent the various dimensional aggregation hierarchies. These hierarchies can then be used in the requisite forecast in order to model cycles of behaviour. Such cycles of behaviour could encompass either temporal, spatial, technological, or spiritual facets. The effect of using behavioural modelling, is that it will stop the long term average forecasts from becoming 'stuck' within a narrow range of values. In order to accomplish mature dimensional learning within your solution, the key asset to build and maintain, is a dimensional aggregation hierarchy table, which contains all the data label relationships. From this, it should be possible to at least partially mine any new data that comes into the AI system. There will usually be a need to have a human in the loop for this game. This human will be validating and correcting any ongoing discovery, 'burying', and re-discovery of dimensions and layers at each dimensionality discovery attempt. Essentially, these attempts should be infrequent, but adjustments should automatically be made to the AI system projections, based on any incoming data in between attempts, via lookups to the dimensional aggregation hierarchy table.

The Dimensionality Discovery Processes

There are three types of 'transactional' data that could be mined:

1. **Well-Labelled Homogeneous Data** - where the rows of data have fully dimensionally layered subjective labels, in columns adjacent to the objective values which are to be directly analysed.
2. **Insufficiently-Labelled Homogeneous Data** - where the rows of data have no labels, or only partially dimensionally layered subjective labels, in columns adjacent to the objective values which are to be directly analysed.
3. **Heterogeneous Data** - where the rows of data contain more than one dimensionality layer in the objective values which are to be directly analysed.

Well-Labelled Homogeneous Data Mining Process

This type of data is almost ready to be dimensionally aggregated because it already contains all the necessary labels, for example, that a row corresponds to a town, which is within a city, which is within a county, etc.). Before aggregating, depending on the solution architecture (i.e. human in-the-loop/out-of-the-loop), it may still be necessary to do a look-up to the dimensional aggregation hierarchy table, in order to validate the label relationships, and to look for any extra, propagatable dimensional layers that were discovered in past analysis.

Insufficiently-Labelled Homogeneous Data Mining Process

This type of data can be treated in the same way as the well-labelled homogeneous data. The only difference is that it will always be necessary to have a human in the loop, in order to supervise the validation and propagation of the dimensional layers attached to the data.

Heterogeneous Data Mining Process

This data type should be uncommon, but it may exist in some database tables.

Preparation Steps

1. To start off, you must import your 'transactional' data into a matrix.
2. Set an appropriate cell calculation (e.g. sum of, weighted average, weighted percentage, etc.).
3. Set the x-axis to the desired objective value that you want to base your mining on.
4. Add a granularity variable to the matrix which will allow you to vary aggregation pool size on the input/x axis. For example, income in $ may be comprised of two $1 payments and two $2 payments, but you could adjust the x-axis dimensional granularity pool size so that these two pairs of values are counted together in two respective cells.
5. Configure the y-axis to aggregate on an output label where you are looking for the existence of dimensionality (e.g. office location, time, etc.).

Discovery Steps

6. Increase granularity pool size variable by a suitable unit of measure (e.g. if your data range is from 1 to 1000, then increments of between 50 and 100 would probably work well to start off with).
7. Execute the matrix.
8. Check the resulting output-axis groupings. If it is a decent size and diversity dataset, there should be many 'lonely' groupings on this axis on the first

cycle. This is not ideal for mining dimensions as the dimensional layer may still be 'buried'.

You must keep repeating the mining cycle until you get as few groupings on the output-axis as possible, but while maintaining an appropriate naturalised percentage deviation between the observations in each grouping, based on the input-axis values. This can be managed by the human user by providing a threshold for naturalised percentage deviation tolerance. After repetitive mining cycles, you will eventually find that the groupings will no longer change at some point, because either they have all grouped into one aggregate dimension, which means there is only one dimensional layer; or the naturalised percentage deviation threshold has been met, which means there are probably multiple dimensional layers in the data set. You can be more sure of multiple dimensional layers, if the sums in some cells have increased substantially, and there are correspondingly, multiple labels aggregated into various groups on the output-axis.

At this point, the dimensional layers should be flagged up to the human user, so that they can validate it by looking up the mapping on the dimensional aggregation hierarchy table. If the dimensional layers are not yet built into the table, the user must carry out a manual mapping exercise (as guidance, the higher or lower the sum value for a given grouping, the higher or lower it is in the dimensional aggregation hierarchy), followed by an update of this table, so that the dimensional layers are ready for use in the system.

The human in-the-loop is necessary, because in some cases, unrelated output labels may have been grouped together by accident, causing a messy dimensionalisation, which needs resolving.

Some clever automated logic can be built into this module of the solution in order to assist the human mapping effort. One example could be a technique which checks lower dimensional layers for input values which necessarily must aggregate into a particular higher layer, for example, because they are the only combination of input values that are available to sum in order to reach the aggregated input value.

Data Mining Dimensional Layer Application

The question here is: Once the dimensional layers have been discovered, how do we integrate them with the correlation learning outputs?

The main output of the correlation games is a correlation describing a gradient relationship between two variables. We know that this is missing one thing i.e. the 'y-intercept'. This quasi y-intercept can be formed based on the AI system's knowledge of the dimensional layers for a particular output variable. Essentially once you have discovered a dimensional layer:

1. You give the user thresholds to decide how much data to use in the y-intercept calculation (e.g. if it's time data, how much historical data to use; and the observations should also be identical to those filtered for use in the corresponding correlation learning analysis).
2. Then based on each of the dimensional layers discovered in the mining process, set the earliest/smallest/least important output value to zero, and then calculate the average movement up or down, per observable interval throughout that particular layer's 'cycle', across the limited dataset. This gives the

human user an output 'trace' which allows them to model the behaviour of a particular dimensional layer.

3. Once you have the average 'behavioural' traces from the previous step, there are two options. Either you automatically add the values of the traces to the appropriate correlation for a given input value, or you simply expose those dimensional layers to the human user, in the form of a tick list, so that they can add the values of the traces, at the click of a button, to the appropriate correlation for a given input variable, therefore allowing them to accurately (through the correlation), and precisely (through the 'behavioural' trace), project the future output variable value.

As a general rule, this final dimensional layer, application process, should be repeated every time you produce a correlation learning game input/output correlation, and vice versa. If you fail to synchronise the two modules in this way, you will end up injecting asymmetric sampling error into your solution, and therefore although it may become more efficient, it will at the same time become less effective.

The Persistent Adaptive Dimensionality Learning Game

In cases where the dimensional cycle interval is irregular, a completely different technique is required, and paramount effort should be invested in code and configuration efficiency, because the solution is very resource intensive. The following technique is a persistent adaptive dimensionality learning technique. Essentially, every time a new observation enters the solution, you have to check the linear correlation of the most recent cycle's dataset, including this new observation. If for more than a user selected number of intervals (not cycle intervals, but rather data output intervals) the linear correlation is changed by more than a user variable acceptable amount, this is a trigger signal indicating that a new cycle 'has' started. In this way, your solution will constantly be analysing either an upwards or a downwards trend for a given variable. At every data output interval, you 'simply' check all the historical upwards cycles (if the current cycle is an upwards cycle) or downwards cycles (if the current cycle is a downwards cycle), within an appropriate historical dataset, and find a user variable number of closest matching cycle 'traces'. To find the closest 'trace' matches, you have to calculate the difference between each recent historical data output interval and its corresponding data output interval for all the similar cycles, as mentioned above. Set all these individual differences to positive values by squaring each one, and then taking the square root of each one. Then you simply average all the naturalised (positive) differences together to get an overall percentage deviation score for that historical cycle in comparison to the current cycle. Then sort for the lowest five overall percentage deviations. Then you take averages of the referentially future portions of these low variance 'traces', and use these averages to project the dimensional manipulation intended by the human user, across as many data output intervals as is appropriate i.e. where all the reference traces can contribute an output value for the averages. These manipulations should then be integrated with all the other major learning games which are currently switched on by the user. If using this technique, remember to include a user input variable to control minimum trend length before any action. One real-world use for this methodology is when you intend to build an AI solution which can trade on a financial market, because as you possibly know, the market can change to a completely different dynamic, at all sorts of cycle intervals. As a warning, this technique is quite slow, and so it may not be ideal for situations where you want the AI to act rapidly as an agent in the world.

The Density Learning Game

The philosophy here, is that when an output variable is subject to competitive forces, it has to be able to model uncertainty. To achieve this, the AI solution needs to be built in a particular way. The overarching methodology is a weighted, asymmetric, mined, Monte Carlo analysis, as follows:

- Over the historical data profile selected for analysis, find all the past points where the actual output variable value was the same as this new current output variable value.
- Construct an array of all the n+1 adjacent output variable values for the set of historical instances of the current output variable value.
- Find your current model's population maximum and minimum output variable values.
- Assign an incremental number to each value in the array.
- You must then combine a higher and lower portion 'likely' value (steps to follow are below), which deals with the specific uncertainty conditions within the real-world system, and within the problem set parameters of the AI solution itself.
- Calculate the first projected output variable value from the combination of the correlation and dimensionality learning games.
- To calculate the lower portion of the density forecast, temporarily restrict the array values to those which are between the projected output variable value, and the population minimum. Then use a random number generator which is limited to the incremental values assigned to this temporary lower portion array, in order to calculate, with uncertainty, a likely future lower portion value (by using the mapping from incremental

assigned value, to the actual output variable value from the historical data).

- To calculate the higher portion of the density forecast, temporarily restrict the array values to those which are between the projected output variable value, and the population maximum. Then use a random number generator which is limited to the incremental values assigned to this temporary higher portion array, in order to calculate, with uncertainty, a likely future higher portion value (by using the mapping from incremental assigned value, to the actual output variable value from the historical data).
- Take the average of the lower and higher portion values, in order to get a realistic and 'likely' projected value. This value should be used instead of the projected value from the combination of just the correlation and dimensionality learning games.

The Limit Learning Game

Every AI system which is acting as an agent in either the physical, technological, or spiritual 'worlds', needs to have some sort of limits placed on it. This is necessary in order to avoid unacceptable risk. These limits are so numerous and nuanced, that I will not bother describing how to implement this limit learning game. I will leave that to the developers to develop what is desired. Needless to say, if you are developing an autonomous car, you want to avoid the risk of a crash. To do this, you would have to place limits on your AI system which can learn the state of the speed, distance, and time equation, in order to know how to mitigate the risk of crashing into surrounding people or objects, and their trajectories, at any point in time and space, while executing it's overarching command to transport a cargo (people or objects) inside itself, to the required destination, via selected route and driving style dynamics. Likewise, if you are developing an AI system which is administering some sort of healthcare procedure to a person, once again you will need to set limits on the possible output values and actions, given the selected style and type dynamics of the procedure, in order to mitigate the risk of causing any unacceptable damage to the patient.

The Blending Game

After describing these learning games, I feel it necessary to add that one would need to somehow integrate the outputs from all of these data analyses. The way to do this, is to give the human user access to percentage variables which allow them to blend the four major learning games together. For example, you could place emphasis on the correlation learning game, by giving it a higher percentage weighting, if you thought that it would be more important in deciding the real-world future. This may be the case when your 'real world' view becomes more stable. You could place emphasis on the dimensionality learning game, by giving it a higher percentage weighting, if you thought that it would be more important in deciding the real-world future. This may be the case when your 'real world' view becomes more cyclical. You could place emphasis on the density learning game, by giving it a higher percentage weighting, if you thought that it would be more important in deciding the real-world future. This may be the case when your 'real world' view becomes more uncertain. Finally, you could place emphasis on the limit learning game, by giving it a higher percentage weighting, if you thought that it would be more important in deciding the real-world future. This may be the case when your 'real world' view becomes more risky. There are a number of other quantitative learning games that must also be blended into the solution in some cases. The full list can be found in a book I have written

called: The Theory of Everything Equation - Projecting Any
Future.

Constructing Variable Hierarchies (Convolutional Neural Networks)

When building a variable hierarchy, look to organise the nodes
in such a way that the ultimate projection variable sits at the
top, with variables having the greatest average
inclination/declination of lines of best fit with respect to this
ultimate projection variable sitting nearer to the top of the
variable hierarchy, and other variables with less
inclined/declined lines of best fit sitting nearer to the bottom of
the variable hierarchy. The variable positions and hierarchy
structure can be optimised further, by carrying out a similar
process for each individual node, reorganising variables until
you reach the bottom end of all the node traces, but it is
important to try and incorporate some form of causal logic into
the final configuration. To implement this technique properly,
you will need to incorporate the use of a weighted average
naturalised inclination/declination (gradient) threshold.

How To Calculate Weighted Gradients:

Element	x	y
Group 1	1	1
Group 2	2	3
Group 3	3	6
Group 4	5	7

Element	Weighted Average
Section 1 (Between Group 1 and 2)	2

Section 2 (Between Group 2 and 3)	3
Section 3 (Between Group 3 and 4)	0.5

Weighted Average Calculation Example: = ({y,Group2} - {y,Group1}) / ({x,Group2} - {x,Group1})

Nota Bene: These weighted average calculation outputs, then need to be averaged in order to get an overall gradient which describes the correlation relationship between the pair of variables... In this case, the average would be 1.83...

Variable weighting is not necessary, and I would argue is more often than not, sub-optimal, in comparison to the reinforcement 'correlations' arising naturally from the previously mentioned techniques (... if there is a good correlation between two variables, they already intrinsically become weighted).

The hierarchy roll-up calculation is simply an average of the lower adjacent layer nodes which are connected to a particular higher layer node. Within each node, the calculation is described in the blending game (above).

The Mature b-AI-by – The Quantum Principle Games

Then there are some slightly 'more' advanced games to 'play'.

The Quantum Tunnelling Game

Can I take 'shortcuts' to my projections, while using less 'power'?

In the case of artificial intelligence, the quantum tunnelling principle describes the quantum phenomenon where a data point passes through a potential barrier that it cannot surmount under the provision of classical software/hardware constraints. The application of this quantum principle is as follows:

Although it's nice to have as many variables as possible stacked up in a cause-effect hierarchy in order to get the most accurate and precise projection, a simpler architecture, i.e. a solution with fewer layers in the cause-effect hierarchy, can be more useful in markets which are changing very quickly, because it means less data processing, and therefore a resulting greater possible frequency of waves of data processing and action, to deal with the higher rate of market change.

The Quantum Uncertainty Game

Can I make 'better' projections, while using less 'data'?

The Heisenberg uncertainty principle states that the position and the velocity of an object cannot both be measured exactly, at the same time, even in theory. The application of this quantum principle is as follows:

Although you want as much granularity of data as possible flowing into the system, the reality is that if you try to process all this, and then perform actions on this, your actions will, in a lot of cases, be sub optimal. The reason is that different modules require a different granularity of detail in order to perform optimal projections. Therefore, if your system is chugging away chewing up data and spitting out recommendations as fast as it possibly can, then the actions will be too short termist. However, if you suck in as much data as you can, but aggregate it into optimal yet changing waves of processing and action, then this will allow for a more long termist action to be made by the system where necessary, to achieve optimisation, and you will retain the fall-back, in some modules that require it, of the highest possible granularity to tackle the more short termist actions. It is recommended that this wave granularity is controlled by the human operator's required intent at any point in time.

The Quantum Entanglement Game

The phenomenon of entanglement causes variables to lose their individuality and in many ways behave as a single entity. This can be seen when they always move in step with each other over an extended period of time. It is advisable to deal with this, by compounding the variables i.e. by compressing the two tandem variables onto the same axis. This can be done through multiplication. This improves the model by simplifying the correlation architecture, and thereby improving speed performance, without sacrificing too much granularity.

The Quantum Precedence Game

The application is to use a setting of weighted distributions 'around' the gradient for a particular variable (most likely towards the top of the variable hierarchy). This adds a certain amount of flexibility to the model, and this configuration should be switched on by the human user when they are confident that the configuration of their model is perfectly set up to act within its environment. In practice, if you have an AI system supporting a human trader on the stock markets, this game would automatically give the AI solution more precedence in deciding buy/sell thresholds, in terms of timings and amounts. This allows it to decide whether to 'overemphasise' it's trading strategy, without the human trader needing to make any changes to thresholds.

The Quantum Predomination Game

Here you must find the 'common denominator' whenever you are winning in a particular environment, so that you can replicate the performance at a later date. For example, by selecting an AI discovered, human trader specific, optimised set of thresholds and inputs, after pre-empting (using technical and fundamental trading techniques) an imminent change to a 'familiar' market, the hybrid trader can quickly switch their trading strategy, without adjusting all the individual thresholds.

The Quantum Clustering Game

The question here is how to deal with a multi-modal observation set. This happens when the observations are segregated, and it causes clustering in the output variable. This clustering of data is a sign that you need to turn the continuous correlation gradient into a discrete correlation gradient, so that the model better fits the data, and so for example, can better project under conditions where the market is segregated.

The Quantum Bending Game

This principle concerns the theory behind deciding to set a correlation to either linear or non-linear. The application is simple. If the data is symmetrical i.e. it follows a straight gradient line in general, even if it is lumpy at points along this gradient line, then you should set that correlation to linear. If however the data is asymmetrical i.e. it doesn't follow a general straight line, but rather seems to curve in any way, then you should set that correlation to non-linear. By playing this game, you will allow the model to better fit the behaviour of the data, and therefore provide better projections.

The Quantum Evolution Game

This principle describes when a gradient reaches a local minima or maxima. If it is a minima or maxima, then the trading algorithm should automatically trade in the direction that it knows the price can only go based on the model and its historical data set.

The Quantum Clashing Game

Beware of clashing i.e. contradictory granularities. There are only a few circumstances where this is useful. Two areas where clashing is useful are as follows:

When you feel like the environment is going to become volatile, you set quantum tunnelling to the higher tiers of the variable hierarchy. At the same time, if you think the environment is going to either fall or rise substantially over the next few minutes, hours, or days (or some other longer than usual time period), set quantum uncertainty to long term e.g. minutely frequency or more. This way for example, if you time it right, you will seriously boost profitability if you are trading the stock markets, however if you time it wrongly, the market may significantly move against your position. This is a very useful tactic, however I would advise that unless you know for sure that the market will move far and for a long time, you should wait until it has already started moving by at least 2% or more. NB: For obvious reasons, this application of quantum clashing should not be used in safety critical missions like automated cars.

Another good use of clashing is when the environment is quite stable i.e. it is trending well, with very little volatility. In this type of environment, you should set quantum uncertainty to shorter terms, in order to capitalise on whatever volatility there is, and quantum tunnelling to the full variable hierarchy so that your model takes full advantage of the price movements that are there in the market because it is taking into account a greater granularity of data from underlying variables. NB: For obvious reasons, this application of quantum clashing should be used in safety critical missions like automated cars.

The Quantum Lifecycle Game

In order to deal with environments where there is a fundamental change in the observed system which the AI system is modelling, i.e. the actual output has changed a lot, you need to speed up learning. This is because the learning is, or is becoming obsolete. The only way to do this is to analyse more variables on each of the fewer relevant observations you have. Then, as the learning improves, you can fine tune, and therefore reduce to the optimum number of variables being analysed per observation, based on those which have more impact on the projection correctly anticipating the actual. This impact can be measured in the form of (statistical) significance.

The Quantum Prolongation Game

Every solution will have to deal with a time dimension. To 'win' this game, you have to analyse the difference between projection and actual, and thereby detect when a particular correlation is 'out-of-date', because the projected output is significantly different from the actual output. When this is the case, the solution, module, or package, should re-run the projection for any future time period using a new set of observations, some of which may have been used in the previous projection.

The Quantum Offsetting Game

When trading a financial market, it is likely that certain types of traders will trade at more or less the same reasoning, incidence, and interval. This gives rise to a market dynamic which I call free-trading (when you are constantly trading fractionally before other traders with similar strategies and tactics), and trap-trading (when you are constantly trading fractionally behind other traders with similar strategies and tactics). You can imagine the consequences of a trader being 'trapped'. Not a good situation! Therefore, every trading solution would need an offsetting variable, which changes the incidence of their AI trading cycle. The reasoning is handled by the various thresholds integrated into the data analysis, configuration, and action, as per described earlier in this document. The interval should be automatically set based on the granularity which a given trader chooses at a particular time, for example, if they are low granularity, then the interval for their instance of the AI solution should be 'acting' on a more long-term basis such as weekly or monthly. Likewise, the various visuals should also default to more long-term, less granular representations of the data.

The Quantum Oracle Game

The concept here, is that a cleverly designed AI solution should probably only take action where the outcome is at least somewhat certain (high confidence), but in comparison, it should simply observe and learn when model certainty is low (low confidence).

www.ingramcontent.com/pod-product-compliance
Lightning Source LLC
Chambersburg PA
CBHW031250050326
40690CB00007B/1030